P9-AGN-697

THE INNER ME

Brimming with creative inspiration, how-to projects, and useful information to enrich your everyday life, Quarto Knows is a favorite destination for those pursuing their interests and passions. Visit our site and dig deeper with our books into your area of interest: Quarto Creates, Quarto Cooks, Quarto Homes, Quarto Lives, Quarto Drives, Quarto Explores, Quarto Gifts, or Quarto Kids.

© 2020 by Quarto Publishing Group USA Inc.

First published in 2020 by Chartwell Books, an imprint of The Quarto Group,
142 West 36th Street, 4th Floor, New York, NY 10018, USA
T (212) 779-4972 F (212) 779-6058 www.QuartoKnows.com

All rights reserved. No part of this journal may be reproduced in any form without written permission of the copyright owners. All images in this journal have been reproduced with the knowledge and prior consent of the artists concerned, and no responsibility is accepted by producer, publisher, or printer for any infringement of copyright or otherwise, arising from the contents of this publication. Every effort has been made to ensure that credits accurately comply with information supplied. We apologize for any inaccuracies that may have occurred and will resolve inaccurate or missing information in a subsequent reprinting of the journal.

Chartwell titles are also available at discount for retail, wholesale, promotional, and bulk purchase. For details, contact the Special Sales Manager by email at specialsales@quarto.com or by mail at The Quarto Group, Attn: Special Sales Manager, 100 Cummings Center Suite 265D, Beverly, MA 01915 USA.

10 9 8 7 6 5 4 3 2

ISBN: 978-0-7858-3912-5

Publisher: Rage Kindelsperger
Creative Director: Laura Drew
Managing Editor: Cara Donaldson
Text: Saskia Lacey
Cover Design & Interior Design: Beth Middleworth

Printed in China

THE INNER ME

A JOURNAL TO CONNECT WITH YOURSELF AND DISCOVER WHAT BRINGS YOU TRUE HAPPINESS

chartwell
books

Getting to Know You

How well do you really know yourself? Do you see yourself as you are, or as you once were?

Use this journal to connect with your inner self. Rediscover your central passions and contemplate what brings you true fulfillment.

The following pages contain hundreds of prompts that encourage you to dream, plan, remember, vent, celebrate, and forgive. As you write, meditate on the accompanying quotes from a variety of individuals from all walks of life. Use the wisdom of their words to guide your responses.

Don't worry about your answers. Just be honest. A truthful review of where you are now is the first step in learning where you want to go next. So, relax, be open, and discover the inner you.

What is your idea of adventure? Describe your greatest adventure.

"Life is either a daring adventure or nothing at all."

—HELEN KELLER

In what small ways are you becoming a better version of yourself?

"For me, becoming isn't about arriving somewhere or achieving a certain aim. I see it instead as forward motion, a means of evolving, a way to reach continuously toward a better self."

—MICHELLE OBAMA

Who are people in your life that encourage self-reflection? How do they help you know yourself better?

"You too? I thought I was the only one."

—C. S. LEWIS

Are you more of a morning person or a night owl? How does this shape your day?

"There is no sunrise so beautiful that it is worth waking me up to see it."
—MINDY KALING

When have you been overwhelmed with wonder?

"The most beautiful thing we can experience is the mysterious. It is the source of all true art and all science."

—ALBERT EINSTEIN

How can you use your talents and passions to help others?

"I have found that among its other benefits, giving liberates the soul of the giver."

—MAYA ANGELOU

In what areas of your life do you need to go slower?

"Anything worth doing is worth doing slowly."

—MAE WEST

What fears are holding you back from achieving your goals?

"Obstacles are those frightful things you see when you take your eyes off the goal."

—HENRY FORD

If you were to design your dream day, what would it look like?

"A schedule defends from chaos and whim. It is a net for catching days."

—ANNIE DILLARD

How can you use your resources (intellectual, emotional, physical) more effectively?

"Do what you can, with what you have, where you are."

—THEODORE ROOSEVELT

What are the greatest lessons you have learned from your mistakes?

"An expert is a person who has made all the mistakes that can be made in a very narrow field."

—NIELS BOHR

When do you laugh the loudest? How would you describe your sense of humor?

"Nothing is worth more than laughter. It is strength to laugh and to abandon oneself, to be light."

—FRIDA KAHLO

In what areas of your life are you a leader? In what areas are you a follower?

"Don't follow the crowd, let the crowd follow you."

—MARGARET THATCHER

Make five small goals for the future. Define each as clearly as you can.

"What can be said at all can be said clearly."

—LUDWIG WITTGENSTEIN

When do you struggle to relate to others? How can you be more empathetic?

"One half of the world cannot understand the pleasures of the other."

—JANE AUSTEN

What do you hope will stand the test of time?

"Truth alone will endure;
all the rest will be swept away
before the tide of time."

—MAHATMA GANDHI

In your opinion, what has a greater influence on a person's actions, their attitude or their situation?

"The greater part of our happiness or misery depends upon our dispositions, and not upon our circumstances."

—MARTHA WASHINGTON

How has your past shaped you in positive and negative ways?

"Even our misfortunes are part of our belongings."

—ANTOINE DE SAINT-EXUPÉRY

Who are three people you can't live without? What makes them essential?

"In a competition of love we'll all share in the victory, no matter who comes first."

–MUHAMMAD ALI

What do you think are some of the benefits of having a positive attitude?

"For myself, I am an optimist—it does not seem to be much use being anything else."

—WINSTON CHURCHILL

Do you live in the gray, or do you see life in black and white?

"A mature person is one who does not think only in absolutes, who is able to be objective even when deeply stirred emotionally."

—ELEANOR ROOSEVELT

In what areas of life do you need to wake up?

"All my work says be serious, be passionate, wake up."

—SUSAN SONTAG

When do you find yourself feeling jealous? What can you learn from these moments?

"Jealousy is a disease; love is a healthy condition."

—ROBERT HEINLEIN

List 10 things you are immensely grateful for.

"When a person doesn't have gratitude, something is missing in his or her humanity. A person can almost be defined by his or her attitude toward gratitude."

—ELIE WIESEL

What habits would you like to discard?

"I knew that good like bad becomes a routine, that the temporary tends to endure, that what is external permeates to the inside, and that the mask, given time, comes to be the face itself."

—MARGUERITE YOURCENAR

Do you think it's dangerous to take yourself too seriously? Why or why not?

"The one important thing I have learned over the years is the difference between taking one's work seriously and taking one's self seriously. The first is imperative and the second is disastrous."

—MARGOT FONTEYN

Who is the wisest person you know? How do they use their wisdom?

"The saddest aspect of life right now is that science gathers knowledge faster than society gathers wisdom."

—ISAAC ASIMOV

Center your focus on the one thing you want to be able to do well. How can you achieve your goal?

"I'd rather learn from one bird how to sing than teach ten thousand stars how not to dance."

—E. E. CUMMINGS

Is there hatred or resentment in your life that you need to let go of?

"I will permit no man to narrow and degrade my soul by making me hate him."

—BOOKER T. WASHINGTON

What do you think are some of your responsibilities as a citizen of the world?

"*You cannot hope to build a better world without improving the individuals.*"

—MARIE CURIE

When are you most independent? When are you most dependent?

"Independence I have long considered as the grand blessing of life, the basis of every virtue."

—MARY WOLLSTONECRAFT

How can you show kindness to others today?

"Three things in human life are important. The first is to be kind. The second is to be kind. And the third is to be kind."

—HENRY JAMES

If your soul had a motto, what would it be? Why?

"This is what my soul is telling me: be peaceful and love everyone."

—MALALA YOUSAFZAI

What is your secret superpower?

"With great power comes great responsibility."

—STAN LEE

Think about your past. What events make sense now that didn't make sense at the time?

"Life can only be understood backwards; but it must be lived forwards."

—SØREN KIERKEGAARD

When has unhappiness motivated you to make changes in your life?

"Were there none who were discontented with what they have, the world would never reach anything better."
—FLORENCE NIGHTINGALE

List three embarrassing moments. Do they make you laugh or cringe?

"All that was great in the past was ridiculed, condemned, combatted, suppressed—only to emerge all the more powerfully, all the more triumphantly from the struggle."

—NIKOLA TESLA

Would you describe yourself as being more conventional or radical? Why?

"Conventionality is not morality. Self-righteousness is not religion. To attack the first is not to assail the last."

—CHARLOTTE BRONTË

When is it best not to fit in with the crowd?

"I cannot and will not cut my conscience to fit this year's fashions."

—LILLIAN HELLMAN

What do you need help with? Who can you ask for help?

"You are never strong enough that you don't need help."

—CESAR CHAVEZ

How can you simplify one area of your life?

"It is vain to do with more what can be done with less."

—WILLIAM OF OCKHAM

What decision are you having trouble making?

"I have learned over the years that
when one's mind is made up, this
diminishes fear; knowing what must
be done does away with fear."

—ROSA PARKS

When does work feel the most rewarding?

"Hard work is its own reward. Integrity is priceless. Art does feed the soul."

—MARCUS SAMUELSSON

Write a silly poem about yourself. Don't think about it too hard!

"You're given the form, but you have to write the sonnet yourself. What you say is completely up to you."

—MADELEINE L'ENGLE

Who have you tried to be in the past? Were you successful?

"Why not be oneself? That is the whole secret of a successful appearance. If one is a greyhound, why try to look like a Pekingese?"

—EDITH SITWELL

What is something unusual that you care deeply about?

"I care deeply about craft: the quality of how something is made and the experience it enables."

—KEVIN SYSTROM

What are small acts of kindness that you appreciate?

"We ourselves feel that what we are doing is just a drop in the ocean. But if the drop was not in the ocean, I think the ocean would be less because of the missing drop."

—MOTHER THERESA

Is there something about yourself that you refuse to admit?

"Being entirely honest with oneself is a good exercise."

—SIGMUND FREUD

What gives you positive energy?

"Life engenders life. Energy creates energy. It is by spending oneself that one becomes rich."

—SARAH BERNHARDT

List three problems you solved recently. Small problems count!

"Success is a collection of problems solved."

—I. M. PEI

Name your fears. Then name why they aren't useful.

"Named must your fear be before banish it you can."

—YODA

When was the last time you cried? What happened?

"Some people say, 'Never let them see you cry.' I say, if you're so mad you could just cry, then cry. It terrifies everyone."

—TINA FEY

How can you turn toward the light today?

"I do so dearly believe that no half-heartedness and no worldly fear must turn us aside from following the light unflinchingly."

—J. R. R. TOLKIEN

When do you feel most at ease?

"The world owes all its onward impulses to men ill at ease. The happy man inevitably confines himself within ancient limits."
—NATHANIEL HAWTHORNE

Are you harder on yourself or others?

"I have multiple ideas per day. The vast majority of these are completely idiotic."

—LUIS VON AHN

When do you feel hopeful?

"'Hope' is the thing with feathers—/ That perches in the soul—"

—EMILY DICKINSON

What superficial fears do you need to let go of?

"When you're 50 you start thinking about things you haven't thought about before. I used to think getting old was about vanity—but actually it's about losing people you love. Getting wrinkles is trivial."

—JOYCE CAROL OATES

What are three true, and truly awesome, things about you?

"Truth is on the march, and nothing will stop it."

—ÉMILE ZOLA

Do you find that life gets easier or more difficult with each passing year?

"The older you get the stronger the wind gets—and it's always in your face."

—PABLO PICASSO

Looking back, what "closed door" was a blessing in disguise?

"When the door closes
you have two choices.
Give up, or keep going.
Let them shut you down
or prove them wrong.
We all start somewhere.
It's where you end up
that counts."

—RIHANNA

When have you felt completely free?

"*All good things are wild and free.*"

—HENRY DAVID THOREAU

Would you describe yourself as confident or insecure? Why?

"A strong leader avoids becoming over-confident to the point of impaired judgment."

—DANIEL LUBETZKY

If you could choose how you die, what would it be?

"You don't get to choose how you're going to die. Or when. You can only decide how you're going to live. Now."

—JOAN BAEZ

Who or what makes you feel like a kid?

"Another belief of mine: that everyone else my age is an adult, whereas I am merely in disguise."

—MARGARET ATWOOD

What would paradise look like to you?

"I had always imagined paradise as a kind of library."

—JORGE LUIS BORGES

Write a plan A, B, and C to reach your biggest goal.

"If Plan A isn't working, I have Plan B, Plan C, and even Plan D."

—VENUS WILLIAMS

Who treats you like you are valuable? What does that look like?

"As human beings, our job in life is to help people realize how rare and valuable each one of us really is, that each of us has something that no one else has—or ever will have—something inside that is unique to all time."

—FRED ROGERS

List 10 things you can get rid of. Then get rid of them!

"To truly cherish the things that are important to you, you must first discard those that have outlived their purpose."

—MARIE KONDO

What makes you the most impatient?

"Patience and shuffle the cards."

—MIGUEL DE CERVANTES

What would you do today even if the world was ending tomorrow?

"Even if I knew that tomorrow the world would go to pieces, I would still plant my apple tree."

—DR. MARTIN LUTHER KING, JR.

Are you procrastinating something important?

"The most difficult thing is the decision to act, the rest is merely tenacity."

—AMELIA EARHART

Describe the biggest surprise of your life.

"Everyone has a plan till they get punched in the mouth."

—MIKE TYSON

When are you ordinary? When are you spectacular?

"We are all ordinary. We are all boring. We are all spectacular. We are all shy. We are all bold. We are all heroes. We are all helpless. It just depends on the day."

—BRAD MELTZER

How do you spread light to others?

"There are two ways of spreading light: to be the candle or the mirror that reflects it."

—EDITH WHARTON

How have you learned from the mistakes of others?

"The most intelligent, most talented people in the world have bad ideas. That's a good thing to learn."

—RASHIDA JONES

Are you a realist or an idealist?

"Those who don't believe in
magic will never find it."
—ROALD DAHL

Describe how a failure led to a success.

"Failure is not the opposite of success, it's part of success."
—ARIANNA HUFFINGTON

List your favorite hobbies. How do they add light to your life?

"A hobby is a happy medium between a passion and a monomania."

—HONORÉ DE BALZAC

What flaws are you thankful to have?

"I do not regret the sufferings and peculiarities of my physical constitution. They have taught me, and continue to teach me, that which I think nothing else could have developed."

—ADA LOVELACE

Do you consider yourself honorable? Why or why not?

"Who sows virtue reaps honor."

—LEONARDO DA VINCI

How is life a gift?

"It's a gift to exist, and with existence comes suffering."
—STEPHEN COLBERT

Do you find it easy to adapt to new situations?

"Don't get set into one form, adapt it and build your own, and let it grow, be like water. Empty your mind, be formless, shapeless—like water."

—BRUCE LEE

How can you enact positive change in your life?

"Change will not come if we wait for
some other person or some other time.
We are the ones we've been waiting for.
We are the change that we seek."

—BARACK OBAMA

Who is the best cook you know? What have they made for you?

"Cooking is revelation and creation . . . not everyone can do it: one must have the gift."

—SIMONE DE BEAUVOIR

What traits have you inherited from your parents?

"I believe that children's souls are the inheritors of historical memory from previous generations."

—HAYAO MIYAZAKI

What three talents do you wish you had?

"It seems to me, when I see nature, that I see it ready-made, completely written— but then, try to do it!"

—CLAUDE MONET

Have you been tamed? Describe why or why not.

"Little minds are tamed and subdued by misfortune; but great minds rise above it."

—WASHINGTON IRVING

How can you enliven the parts of your life that have become mundane?

"I don't want to get to the end of my life and find that I just lived the length of it. I want to live the width of it as well."

—DIANE ACKERMAN

Do you prefer small towns or big cities?

"When I first moved to New York, someone who thought they knew more than I did said: 'You have to always look like you know where you're going when you get out of the subway.'"

—MAYA RUDOLPH

What's the craziest thing you have done for love?

"Whenever I get married,
I start buying *Gourmet*
magazine. I think of it as my
own personal bride's disease."
—NORA EPHRON

How do you see yourself first and foremost?

"I am a mother first, then a CEO and then a wife."

—INDRA NOOYI

Do you prefer a quiet night alone or a noisy night out?

"Anything for a quiet life."
—THOMAS MIDDLETON

In what areas of your life do you need to push yourself?

"Do not go gentle into that good night, / Old age should burn and rave at close of day; / Rage, rage against the dying of the light."

—DYLAN THOMAS

Which books have had the greatest impact on your life?

"*Whenever you read a good book, somewhere in the world a door opens to allow in more light.*"

—VERA NAZARIAN

Do you prefer savory or sweet food? Describe your favorite dish.

"There is no love sincerer than the love of food."

—GEORGE BERNARD SHAW

What day would you like to relive again and again?

"I'm just trying to look at something without blinking, to see what it is like, or it could have been like, and how that had something to do with the way we live now."

—TONI MORRISON

If you could dance with anyone, who would it be? Why?

"We look at the dance to impart the sensation of living in an affirmation of life, to energize the spectator into keener awareness of the vigor, the mystery, the humor, the variety, and the wonder of life."

—MARTHA GRAHAM

How would you describe your current physical health?

"Better to hunt in fields, for health unbought, / Than fee the doctor for a nauseous draught."

—JOHN DRYDEN

How can you use your past experience to avoid future trouble?

"We hope all danger may be overcome; but to conclude that no danger may ever arise would itself be extremely dangerous."

—ABRAHAM LINCOLN

Create five nonsense words that perfectly describe your life. Then write their definitions.

"Life is Supercalifragilisticexpialidocious."

—JULIE ANDREWS

What do you find boring?

"Why doth one man's yawning make another yawn?"

—ROBERT BURTON

What culture would you like to learn more about?

"I always felt I was a foreigner."

—MADELEINE ALBRIGHT

Share the memory behind your favorite personal photograph.

"When words become unclear, I shall focus with photographs. When images become inadequate, I shall be content with silence."

—ANSEL ADAMS

When you were a child, who did you want to become?

"Oh never another dream can be / Like that early dream of ours, / When the fairy Hope lay down to sleep, / Like a child, among the flowers."

—LETITIA ELIZABETH LANDON

What kind of first impression do you think you make? Is it truthful to who you are?

"When you meet somebody for the first time, you're not meeting them. You're meeting their representative."

—CHRIS ROCK

In general, do you prefer variety or routine?

> *"I like being able to do something really big, and then something tiny, and something independent, and something not."*
>
> —BEN WHISHAW

When have you underestimated yourself?

"Never limit yourself because of others' limited imagination; never limit others because of your own limited imagination"
—MAE JEMISON

Who do you know whose happiness makes them beautiful?

"Happy people are beautiful. They become like a mirror and they reflect that happiness."

—DREW BARRYMORE

Who are people you consider to be kindred spirits? They can be famous or otherwise.

"I never felt like a part of the majority."

—SERGEY BRIN

Would you describe yourself as focused or distracted?

"Always remember, your focus determines your reality."
—GEORGE LUCAS

What are you passionate enough to protest for?

"We shall continue to picket because it is our right."

—ROSE WINSLOW

List your favorite lowbrow pleasures.

"But I do nothing that I don't like, such as 'inventing' up to the arty or 'down' to the corny. I happen to relish a certain type of corn."

—FRED ASTAIRE

How do you wish you were more like your childhood self?

"If children are different from us, they are more spontaneous. Grown-up lives have become overlaid with dross."

—MAURICE SENDAK

If your life could transmit one message, what would it be?

"My message is always felicidad—happiness."

—CELIA CRUZ

What activity makes you feel like you're flying?

"*Imagination is the highest kite that can fly.*"

—LAUREN BACALL

Which of your friends or acquaintances is your polar opposite? Describe how.

"I like friends who have independent minds because they tend to make you see problems from all angles."

—NELSON MANDELA

What kind of movie would your life be?

"Life's like a movie; write your own ending, keep believing, keep pretending."

—JIM HENSON

How are you different from your parents?

> *"Everything I do now is a product of my ancestry."*
>
> —DIANA AL-HADID

Which risks are you glad you took?

"I have continuously taken risks in my career and in the process reinvented myself many times."

—VINOD DHAM

What are you really terrible at?

"Knowing what you cannot do is more important than knowing what you can do. In fact, that's good taste."

—LUCILLE BALL

List your favorite childhood books.

"That's what books are for...to travel without moving an inch."
—JHUMPA LAHIRI

Who are your heroes? Why do you think they are great?

*"If I have seen further,
it is by standing upon
the shoulders of giants."*
—SIR ISAAC NEWTON

Where would you most like to live?

"*Adventure must start with running away from home.*"
—WILLIAM BOLITHO

What journey have you enjoyed more than the destination?

"*A good traveler has no fixed plans, and is not intent on arriving.*"

—LAO TZU

In what ways have you been blessed?

"Whenever you feel like criticizing anyone ... just remember that all the people in this world haven't had the advantages that you've had."

—F. SCOTT FITZGERALD

List your most basic needs (aside from food, water, and sleep).

"I myself was born with an enormous need for affection and a terrible need to give it."

—AUDREY HEPBURN

Describe the greatest party you've ever been to.

"Good parties
create a temporary
youthfulness."
—MASON COOLEY

Are you more of a dog or a cat person? Why?

"It's funny how dogs and cats know the inside of folks better than other folks do, isn't it?"

—ELEANOR PORTER

Make a list of things you don't need to worry about.

"Shed no tear! O shed no tear! / The flower will bloom another year."

—JOHN KEATS

What type of qualities do you look for in a friend?

"So let's peek behind the curtain and hail the others like us. The open-faced sandwiches who take risks and live big and smile with all of their teeth. These are the people I want to be around."

—AMY POEHLER

Do you consider yourself generous? Why or why not?

"You give but little when you give of your possessions. It is when you give of yourself that you truly give."

—KAHLIL GIBRAN

What qualities would you like to absorb from other people?

"Acting is a question of absorbing other people's personalities and adding some of your own experiences."

—PAUL NEWMAN

Who do you have trouble forgiving?

"We have all a chance of meeting with some pity, some tenderness, some charity, when we are dead: it is the living only who cannot be forgiven—the living only from whom men's indulgence and reverence are held off, like the rain by the hard east wind."

—GEORGE ELIOT

What have you given up on that you would like to pursue again?

"What is harder than rock, or softer than water? Yet soft water hollows out hard rock. Persevere."

—OVID

Describe a crossroads you are facing right now.

"Two roads diverged in a wood, and I— / I took the one less traveled by, / And that has made all the difference."
—ROBERT FROST

What is the strangest place you have visited?

"Basically, I believe the world is a jungle, and if it's not a bit of a jungle in the home, a child cannot possibly be fit to enter the outside world."

—BETTE DAVIS

Are you more of a turtle or a hare? Explain.

"Now, here you see, it takes all the running you can do, to keep in the same place. If you want to get somewhere else, you must run at least twice as fast as that!"

—LEWIS CARROLL

Who would play you in a movie about your life?

"When you make the movie about this whole NBC late night fiasco, I'd like to be played by Academy-Award winning actress Tilda Swinton."

—CONAN O'BRIEN

Describe your greatest childhood accomplishment.

"Even as kids, we're capable of doing so much."
—MIKAILA ULMER

What great success didn't feel as great as you thought it would?

"Winning is many things, but it is never the thing you thought it would be."

—MIRANDA JULY

Who or what remains a mystery to you?

"He who is in love is wise and is becoming wiser, sees newly every time he looks at the object beloved, drawing from it with his eyes and his mind those virtues which it possesses."

—RALPH WALDO EMERSON

In general, do you prefer stories with happy or sad endings?

"I don't like a sad ending."
—DWAYNE JOHNSON

Name the top three things that stress you out.

"*The body registers stress, whether good or bad, in the same way. So if it's super exciting or super traumatizing, your body is in equal distress. Though I would choose excitement over trauma every day.*"
—LUPITA NYONG'O

How important is financial wealth to you?

"I'm a revolutionary, money
means nothing to me."
—FRÉDÉRIC CHOPIN

How do you react in an emergency?

"The winds will blow their own freshness into you, and the storms their energy."

—JOHN MUIR

What freedom do you cherish above all others?

"Lock up your libraries if you like; but there is no gate, no lock, no bolt that you can set upon the freedom of my mind."

—VIRGINIA WOOLF

Whose death has had the greatest impact on your life?

"It is human nature to look away from illness. We don't enjoy a reminder of our own fragile mortality."

—ROGER EBERT

Vent about a particularly annoying authority figure from your past.

"Choose only one master—Nature."

—REMBRANDT

What keeps you up at night?

"I couldn't go to sleep in the evening without looking at the stars and wondering what those little points of light were."
—ADRIANA OCAMPO

What's on your to-read list? How do you hope these books will improve your life?

"Reading is at the heart of all achievement."

—PLEASANT ROWLAND

Describe your earliest memory. How has it shaped you?

"A little child born yesterday / A thing on mother's milk and kisses fed."

—HOMER

Are you mostly an introvert or an extrovert? Explain why.

"Deep inside, I am a shy man. And in the presence of colorful characters, I am a clam. I never try to out-eccentric the eccentrics!"

—ALFRED HITCHCOCK

Are you trying to prove something to yourself or others? What is it?

"Once you're lucky; twice you're good. You have to do it a second time."

—MIRIAM NAFICY

Do you have an easy time sharing your feelings? Why or why not?

"I had to resign myself, many years ago, that I'm not too articulate when it comes to explaining how I feel about things. But my music does it for me, it really does."

—DAVID BOWIE

If you were an animal, what animal would you be?

"Life is a beautiful, magnificent thing, even to a jellyfish."

—CHARLIE CHAPLIN

Make a list of things you'd be proud to accomplish today.

"You control your day. You have 24 hours. What will you do with it?"

—LILLY SINGH

What questions do you wish other people would ask you?

"Here I am, in the genuine flesh. Are you going to ask me about my favorite breakfast cereal again?"

—ANNIE BARROWS

Do you consider yourself artistic?

"I don't have to be a tortured artist to be interesting."

—TAIKA WAITITI

Whose perspective do you need on a current difficulty?

"I find it fascinating that you can look at the same problem from different perspectives."

—MARYAM MIRZAKHANI

How has your style evolved over the course of your life?

"You can have anything you want in life if you dress for it."

—EDITH HEAD

Do you need to set boundaries with your technology use? Why or why not?

"Just put that phone away and be where you are."

—MICHAEL CHABON

Who or what do you think is totally overrated?

"People who shop in health food stores never look healthy."

—AMY SEDARIS

Do you have important young ones in your life? Who are they?

"Although I have never had children of my own, and cannot say I had a particularly marvelous childhood, perhaps I can say I am still like a child myself. Part of me, I guess, never grew up."

—GYO FUJIKAWA

Summarize your political beliefs.

"There is no one who ever acts honestly
in the administration of states, nor
any helper who will save any one who
maintains the cause of the just."

—PLATO

How close are you with your immediate family?

"A dysfunctional family is any family with more than one person in it."

—MARY KARR

What do you hope to live long enough to see?

"I hope I live long enough to be the great-grandmother of all agitators."

—MOTHER JONES

What's the nicest thing someone has said to you?

"It is not for minds like ours to give or to receive flattery; yet the praises of sincerity have ever been permitted to the voice of friendship."

—LORD BYRON

Describe your cultural background. In what ways has it shaped you?

"Whenever two cultures meet, it's the little things that make a big difference."

—YO-YO MA

Who was the most influential person in your childhood?

"My mother was my whole world, I learned risk-taking from her."

—MAZIE HIRONO

Do you have any phobias? What are they?

"What terrified me will terrify others; and I need only describe the spectre which had haunted my midnight pillow."

—MARY SHELLEY

What do you need to give yourself more credit for?

"The most common way people give up their power is by thinking they don't have any."

—ALICE WALKER

In what areas of your life are you making progress, slowly but surely?

"It does not matter how slowly you go as long as you do not stop."

—CONFUCIUS

Describe your greatest adventure or vacation.

"An American has not seen the United States until he has seen Mardi Gras in New Orleans."

—MARK TWAIN

What smells do you associate with contentment?

"Perfume is medicine."

—SOPHIA GROJSMAN

What do you wish you would have started a year ago?

"*A year from now you may wish you had started today.*"

—KAREN LAMB

How do you react when things don't go your way?

"Life is 10% what happens to me
and 90% of how I react to it."
—CHARLES SWINDOLL

What are your favorite subjects to study?

"Studies serve for delight, for ornament, and for ability."
—FRANCIS BACON

When was the last time you were truly happy?

"I urge you to please notice when you are happy, and exclaim or murmur or think at some point, 'If this isn't nice, I don't know what is.'"

—KURT VONNEGUT

Do you consider yourself a trendsetter? Why or why not?

"You have to be important to be copied."

—AMALIA HERNÁNDEZ

Describe one of your deeply held beliefs.

"You don't have to change yourself
or your beliefs to be successful."

—HALIMA ADEN

Do you mostly accept or mostly oppose your current circumstances?

"I accept the universe."

—MARGARET FULLER

Which quote from this book do you disagree with? Describe your reasons.

"A lot of the time the experts, the people who are supposed to be able to tell you what to do, will tell you that you can't do something even when you know you can."

—MARK ZUCKERBERG

What did you learn from your last project, work or otherwise?

"There will come a time when you believe everything is finished. That will be the beginning."
—LOUIS L'AMOUR

What have you found to be a waste of time?

"Time is the coin of your life. It is the only coin you have, and only you can determine how it will be spent. Be careful lest you let other people spend it for you."

—CARL SANDBURG

What are some common misconceptions that others have about you?

"God, I'm glad I'm not me."

—BOB DYLAN

Is there a way to change the things that make you miserable?

"Be miserable. Or motivate yourself. Whatever has to be done, it's always your choice."

—WAYNE DYER

What does your best look like at this moment?

"The thing that I do best is 'Be here. Be now.'"

—OPRAH WINFREY

How many close friends do you have?

"*You can make more friends in two months by being interested in them, than in two years by making them interested in you.*"

—DALE CARNEGIE

What things do you find beautiful that other people find ordinary?

"Find things beautiful as much as you can, most people find too little beautiful."

—VINCENT VAN GOGH

Is there a connection between success and passion?

"People are more likely to be successful if they have a passion for what they do."

—URSULA BURNS

What beauty have you found in your dark times?

"*Don't cry when the sun is gone, because the tears won't let you see the stars.*"

—VIOLETA PARRA

What first steps toward peace can you take today?

"When the power of love
overcomes the love of power
the world will know peace."
—JIMI HENDRIX

In what areas do you consider yourself an expert?

"Knowledge is something nobody can steal."

—RAZIA JAN

How can you create joy in your life and the lives of others?

"Life will bring you pain all by itself.
Your responsibility is to create joy."
—MILTON ERICKSON

Are you more silly or serious?

"*If people did not sometimes do silly things, nothing intelligent would ever get done.*"

—LUDWIG WITTGENSTEIN

Do you often question the status quo? Why or why not?

"If someone says 'No'
to me, I say: 'Why?'"
—ANNE WOJCICKI

When do you feel the least self-conscious?

"I want to sing like the birds sing, not worrying about who hears or what they think."

—RUMI

How can you make peace with the unknown?

"We need something new. We can't predict what that will be or when we will find it because if we knew that, we would have found it already!"

—STEPHEN HAWKING

What does the word grace mean to you?

"I do not at all understand the mystery of grace—only that it meets us where we are but does not leave us where it found us."

—ANNE LAMOTT